Korean Words with Cat Memes 1/5

Copyright © 2016 Min Kim

All rights reserved. No part of this book may be reproduced, copied, scanned, or distributed in any form without written permission from the author.

First Edition: December 2016

ISBN: 978-1542678124

www.easy-korean.com

# Contents

| | |
|---|---|
| Preface | 3 |
| 1. Basic Pronouns | 7 |
| 2. People | 13 |
| 3. Travel | 41 |
| 4. Languages | 54 |
| 5. Things | 70 |
| 6. Auto | 79 |
| 7. Hospitals & Pharmacies | 93 |
| Chapter 1 Self Quiz & Answers | 99 |
| Chapter 2 Self Quiz & Answers | 103 |
| Chapter 3 Self Quiz & Answers | 122 |
| Chapter 4 Self Quiz & Answers | 132 |
| Chapter 5 Self Quiz & Answers | 144 |
| Chapter 6 Self Quiz & Answers | 151 |
| Chapter 7 Self Quiz & Answers | 162 |
| Hangul Pronunciations | 167 |
| Word Categories | 168 |
| More Information | 171 |
| Last Words | 172 |

# Preface

What is the most important thing when it comes to learning a new language? The answer is sound, sound, sound. Think of how a baby learns to speak for the first time. Does he learn to read and write first? Not really. He just spends all day on his back, listening to various sounds his parents make to him. And it works. It just does. We are not exactly sure how and why though. But one thing is very clear. Listening is the best way of learning new languages and learning Korean is no exception.

So what good is a book when you need sound to listen to? Well, this book tells you what to listen for. In other words, well... words. After all, a language is made up of words. We just have to figure out what they mean (a.k.a. comprehension) and how to place them in right orders (a.k.a. grammar).

Ideally speaking, a beginner should know meanings of 500 to 1,000 words before moving on to the next level. Each book in this series contains at least 250 words in Korean. That means you don't have to memorize every single word in each book. Just pick the words you like to learn first. Start with the easiest ones. Make it as easy and fun as possible. (Nobody said studying has to be painful for it to be effective. In fact, it is usually the other way around.)

Once you have memorized more than 500 words, you will be able to listen to Korean sentences and understand them a little bit. When you reach that level, you should go ahead and tackle Korean grammar as well as Hangul, the Korean Alphabet.

## Memorize Words the Easy Way

The words in this book are organized by English words and not by Korean words. Why, you ask? The short answer is because it works better this way. Now here comes the long answer.

Let's say you're trying to learn what '나무 (namu)' means. When you hear the word, "nah-moo," your brain does not know what to make of it. So the brain simply ignores the sound and processes it as just some random noise, which it is not. But if you look at the word 'tree' first, your brain will light up the brain cell for that particular word. Now the brain is ready to make a connection between 'tree' and '나무 (namu)' and stores it in your memory. Pretty cool, isn't it?

## Words Handpicked for Beginners

Every word in this book was selected carefully to fit the needs of a new learner. More than a thousand entries are divided into five books and 35 categories. Most of the words are nouns since they are the most essential words for beginners. The most commonly used words from other parts of speech (verbs, adjectives, etc.) are also covered in Korean Words with Cat Memes 2/5 to Korean Words with Cat Memes 5/5.

## Cat Memes! Because Why Not?

To make studying more fun, "educational" cat memes are included in this series. (Every book contains unique memes.) The memes were made with photos of two house cats, Soomba and Zorro. In case anyone is curious, here is a little bit of information on who they are.

**Soomba** (숨바꼭질)

Female

Loves tuna and chicken

Knows how to control her owner

**Zorro** (조로)

Male

Loves special treats

Toilet-trained, can open doors

## Before We Begin

1. The word order of Korean sentences is different from the word order of English sentences. For example, the sentence "The car hit me" would be written as "The car me hit" in Korean. (This sentence can also become "Me hit," because the subject is often omitted.)

2. The Korean language heavily depends on nouns. English words that belong in other parts of speech may be expressed as nouns in Korean.

3. Technically speaking, the Korean words used inside the memes may or may not be grammatically correct. This was done to make things not too complicated for beginners.

# 1. Basic Pronouns

**he**

1. 그 (geu)

Sounds like "geu"

ex. 그는 어디 갔어? = Where did he go?

(Geu-neu nuh-dee gah-ssuh?)


**I**

1. 나 (nah)

Sounds like "nah"

ex. 나는 유럽에서 왔어요. = I'm from Europe.

(Nah-neu nyou-ruh-beh-suh wah-ssuh-yoh.)

## pronoun

1. 대명사 (daemyungsa)

Sounds like "dae-myuhng-sah"

ex. 대명사는 잘 안 쓰인다. = Pronouns are not used a lot.

(Dae-myuhng-sah-neun jah rahn sseu-een-dah.)


## she

1. 그녀 (geu-nyeo)

Sounds like "geu-nyuh"

ex. 그녀는 집에 갔습니다. = She went home.

(Geu-nyuh-neun jee-beh gah-sseub-nee-dah.)

## that

1. 저 (jeo), as in "that person"

Sounds like "juh"

ex. 저 건물인가요? = Is it that building?

(Juh guhn-moo-reen-gah-yoh?)


2. 저것 (jeogeot), as in "that means"

Sounds like "juh-guht"

ex. 저것은 무엇입니까? = What is that?

(Juh-guh-seun moo-uh-sheeb-nee-ggah?)


## there

1. 저기 (jeogi)

Sounds like "juh-ghee"

ex. 저기로 가야해. = We need to go there.

(Juh-ghee-roh gah-yah-hae.)


## these

1. 이것들 (igeotdeul)

Sounds like "ee-guh-ddeul"

ex. 이것들은 뭐예요? = What are these?

(Ee-guh-ddeu-reun mwuh-yeah-yoh?)

## they

1. 그들 (geudeul)

Sounds like "geu-deul"

ex. 그들을 만나지 못 했다. = I could not meet them.

(Geu-deu-reul mahn-nah-jee moh taet-ddah.)

## this

1. 이 (i), as in "this pencil"

Sounds like "ee"

ex. 이 책은 재미있네요. = This book is fun.

(Ee chae-geun jae-mee-eet-neh-yoh.)

2. 이것 (igeot), as in "this is"

Sounds like "ee-guht"

ex. 이것 좀 보세요. = Look at this.

(Ee-guht jjohm boh-seh-yoh.)

### those

1. 저것들 (jeogeotdeul)

Sounds like "juh-guht-ddeul"

ex. 저것들은 비싸다. = Those are expensive.

(Juh-guht-ddeu-reun bee-ssah-dah.)


### we

1. 우리 (wuri)

Sounds like "woo-ree"

ex. 우리 뭐 먹을까? = What should we eat?

(Woo-ree mwuh muh-geul-ggah?)

## you

1. 너 (neo), informal/casual form

Sounds like "nuh"

ex. 너 지금 어디야? = Where are you right now?

(Nuh jee-geum uh-dee-yah?)


2. 당신 (dangshin), formal/honorific form

Sounds like "dahng-sheen"

ex. 당신을 존경합니다. = I respect you.

(Dahng-shee-neul john-gyuhng-hahb-nee-dah.)

# 2. People

### adult

1. 성인 (seongin)

Sounds like "suhng-een"

ex. 19세부터 성인입니다. = You are an adult starting at 19.

(Sheeb-ggoo-seh-boo-tuh suhng-ee-neeb-nee-dah.)


### age

1. 나이 (nai)

Sounds like "nah-ee"

ex. 나이가 어떻게 되세요? = What is your age?

(Nah-ee-gah uh-dduh-keh dweh-seh-yoh?)

## Asian

1. 아시아인 (asiain)

Sounds like "ah-shee-ah-een"

ex. 저 사람은 아시아인입니다. = That person is Asian.

(Juh sah-rah-meu nah-shee-ah-ee-neeb-nee-dah.)

## aunt

1. 큰어머니 (keuneomeoni), wife of father's older brother

Sounds like "keu-nuh-muh-nee"

ex. 큰어머니는 지금 바쁘세요. = Aunt is busy right now.

(Keu-nuh-muh-nee-neun jee-geum bah-bbeu-seh-yoh.)

2. 작은어머니 (jakeuneomeoni), wife of father's y. brother

Sounds like "jah-geu-nuh-muh-nee"

ex. 작은어머니를 찾고 있어요. = I'm looking for my aunt.

(Jah-geu-nuh-muh-nee-reul chaht-ggoh ee-ssuh-yoh.)


3. 고모 (gomo), father's sister

Sounds like "goh-moh"

ex. 고모한테 전화 드려라. = Call your aunt.

(Goh-moh-hahn-teh juhn-hwah deu-ryuh-rah.)


4. 이모 (imo), mother's sister

Sounds like "ee-moh"

ex. 이모, 이리 오세요. = Aunt, please come here.

(Ee-moh, ee-ree oh-seh-yoh.)


5. 외숙모 (wesukmo), wife of mother's brother

Sounds like "weh-soong-moh"

ex. 외숙모가 책을 주셨어요. = Aunt gave me a book.

(Weh-soong-moh-gah chae-geul joo-shuh-ssuh-yoh.)

## baby

1. 아기 (agi), human baby

Sounds like "ah-ghee"

ex. 아기가 울고 있어요. = The baby is crying.

(Ah-ghee-gah wool-goh ee-ssuh-yoh.)


2. 새끼 (saeggi), animal baby

Sounds like "sae-gghee"

ex. 원숭이가 새끼를 찾았다. = The monkey found its baby.

(Wuhn-soong-ee-gah sae-gghee-reul chah-jaht-ddah.)


## barber

1. 이발사 (ibalsa)

Sounds like "ee-bahl-ssah"

ex. 이발사가 물어봅니다. = The barber is asking a question.

(Ee-bahl-ssah-gah moo-ruh-bohb-nee-dah.)


## black (people)

1. 흑인 (heukin)

Sounds like "heu-gheen"

ex. 카일은 흑인이니? = Is Kyle black?

(Kah-ee-reun heu-ghee-nee-nee?)

## boy

1. 소년 (sonyeon), young man

Sounds like "soh-nyuhn"

ex. 소년이 다섯 명 있다. = There are five boys.

(Soh-nyuh-nee dah-suht myuhng eet-ddah.)

2. 남자 (namja), male gender

Sounds like "nahm-jah"

ex. 남자 화장실이 어디 있나요? = Where is boy's bathroom?

(Nahm-jah hwah-jahng-shee-ree uh-dee eet-nah-yoh?)

# brother

1. 형 (hyeong), man's older brother or male friend

Sounds like "hyuhng"

ex. 형, 지금 어디야? = Brother, where are you right now?

(Hyuhng, jee-geu muh-dee-yah?)


2. 오빠 (obba), woman's older brother or male friend

Sounds like "oh-bbah"

ex. 너희 오빠는 무슨 스타일? = Your brother is what style?

(Nuh-hee oh-bbah-neun moo-seun seu-tah-eel?)


3. 남동생 (namdongsaeng), younger brother

Sounds like "nahm-dohng-saeng"

ex. 제 남동생이에요. = This is my younger brother.

(Jeh nahm-dohng-saeng-ee-eh-yoh.)

## child

1. 어린이 (eorini), young person before puberty

Sounds like "uh-ree-nee"

ex. 어린이는 못 들어옵니다. = Children cannot come in.

(Uh-ree-nee-neun moht ddeu-ruh-ohb-nee-dah.)


2. 아이 (ai), kid/baby/young person

Sounds like "ah-ee"

ex. 제 아이 어디에 있어요? = Where is my child?

(Jeh ah-ee uh-dee-eh ee-ssuh-yoh?)

## citizen

1. 국민 (gukmin)

Sounds like "goong-meen"

ex. 그는 국민이 아닙니다. = He is not a citizen.

(Geu-neun goong-mee-nee ah-neeb-nee-dah.)

## cop

1. 경찰 (gyeongchal)

Sounds like "gyuhng-chahl"

ex. 네, 저는 경찰입니다. = Yes, I am a cop.

(Neh, juh-neun gyuhng-chah-reeb-nee-dah.)

## cousin

1. 사촌 (sachon)

Sounds like "sah-chohn"

ex. 얘는 내 사촌 동생이야. = This is my younger cousin.

(Ae-neun nae sah-chohn dohng-saeng-ee-yah.)

## dad

1. 아빠 (abba)

Sounds like "ah-bbah"

ex. 아빠는 지금 운전 중이세요. = Dad is driving right now.

(Ah-bbah-neun jee-geum woon-juhn joong-ee-seh-yoh.)

# daughter

1. 딸 (ttal)

Sounds like "ddahl"

ex. 저희는 딸만 하나 있습니다. = We have just one daughter.

(Juh-hee-neun ddahl-mahn hah-nah ee-sseub-nee-dah.)

# father

1. 아버지 (abeoji)

Sounds like "ah-buh-jee"

ex. 아버지, 이쪽이에요. = Father, this way.

(Ah-buh-jee, ee-jjoh ghoo oh-yoh.)

# female, the

1. 여성 (yeoseong)

Sounds like "yuh-suhng"

ex. 여성을 위한 방입니다. = This is a room for the female.

(Yuh-suhng-eul wee-hahn bahng-eeb-nee-dah.)

## firefighter

1. 소방관 (sobanggwan)

Sounds like "soh-bahng-gwahn"

ex. 그의 직업은 소방관이다. = His job is a firefighter.

(Geu-eui jee-guh-beun soh-bahng-gwah-nee-dah.)


## first name

1. 이름 (ireum)

Sounds like "ee-reum"

ex. 그의 이름은 민호이다. = His first name is Minho.

(Geu-eui ee-reu-meun meen-hoh-ee-dah.)

## foreigner

1. 외국인 (wegukin)

Sounds like "weh-goo-gheen"

ex. 혹시 외국인이세요? = Are you a foreigner?

(Hohg-ssee weh-goo-ghee-nee-seh-yoh?)

## friend

1. 친구 (chingu)

Sounds like "cheen-goo"

ex. 얘는 내 친구야. = This person is my friend.

(Ae-neun nae cheen-goo-yah.)

## gender

1. 성 (seong)

Sounds like "suhng"

ex. 성이 어떻게 되십니까? = What is your gender?

(Suhng-ee uh-dduh-keh dweh-sheeb-nee-ggah?)

MY 'SUHNG' IS BETTER

THAN ZORRO'S 'SUHNG'

## girl

1. 소녀 (sonyeo), young woman

Sounds like "soh-nyuh"

ex. 소녀는 눈물을 흘렸다. = The girl shed tears.

(Soh-nyuh-neun noon-moo-reul heul-lyuht-ddah.)

2. 여자 (yeoja), female gender

Sounds like "yuh-jah"

ex. 남자가 아니라 여자예요. = I am a woman and not a man.

(Nahm-jah-gah ah-nee-rah yuh-jah-yeah-yoh.)

# granddaughter

1. 손녀 (sonnyeo)

Sounds like "sohn-nyuh"

ex. 손녀가 전화를 했다. = My granddaughter called me.

(Sohn-nyuh-gah juhn-hwah-reul haet-ddah.)

# grandparents

1. 할아버지 할머니 (halabeoji halmeoni)

Sounds like "hah-rah-buh-jee hahl-muh-nee"

ex. 할아버지 할머니 오셨다. = Your grandparents are here.

(Hah-rah-buh-jee hahl-muh-nee oh-shuht-ddah.)

# grandson

1. 손자 (sonja)

Sounds like "sohn-jah"

ex. 손자가 몇 살이에요? = How old is your grandson?

(Sohn-jah-gah myuht ssah-ree-eh-yoh?)

# human

1. 인간 (ingan)

Sounds like "een-gahn"

ex. 인간답게 행동해. = Start acting like a human.

(Een-gahn-dahb-ggeh haeng-dohng-hae.)

## husband

1. 남편 (nampyeon)

Sounds like "nahm-pyuhn"

ex. 남편이랑 같이 있어요. = I am with my husband.

(Nahm-pyuh-nee-rahng gah-chee ee-ssuh-yoh.)

## kid

1. 애 (ae), general form

Sounds like "ae"

ex. 애 좀 잠시 봐 줘. = Watch this kid for a minute.

(Ae johm jahm-shee bwah jwuh.)

2. 아이 (ai), alternative form

Sounds like "ah-ee"

ex. 아이랑 같이 밥 먹고 있어. = I'm eating with my kid.

(Ah-ee-rahng gah-chee bahb muhg-ggoh ee-ssuh.)

## king

1. 왕 (wang)

Sounds like "wahng"

ex. 그는 나중에 왕이 되었다. = Later, he became a king.

(Geu-neun nah-joong-eh wahng-ee dweh-uht-ddah.)

## last name

1. 성 (seong)

Sounds like "suhng"

ex. 성은 무조건 앞에 와. = The last name always goes first.

(Suhng-eun moo-joh-gguh nah-peh wah.)

## male, the

1. 남성 (namseong)

Sounds like "nahm-suhng"

ex. 남성한테 인기가 많아요. = It is popuplar among the male.

(Nahm-suhng-hahn-teh een-gghee-gah mah-nah-yoh.)

## man

1. 남자 (namja)

Sounds like "nahm-jah"

ex. 그 남자는 노래를 잘해. = The man is a good singer.

(Geu nahm-jah-neun noh-rae-reul jahl-hae.)

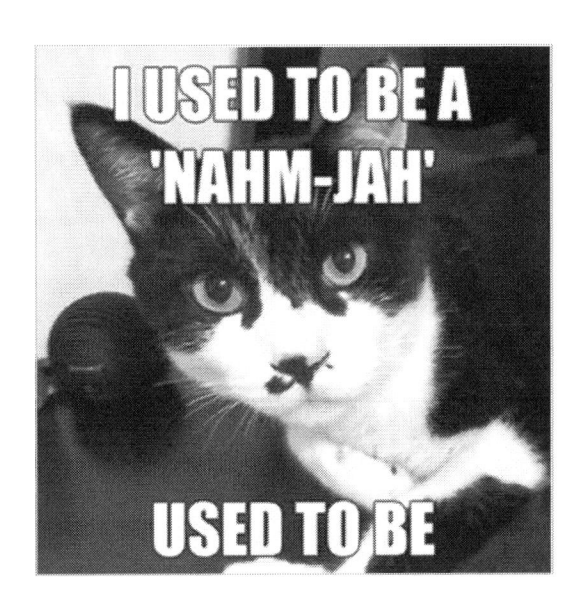

## marriage

1. 결혼 (gyeolhon)

Sounds like "gyuhl-hohn"

ex. 오늘 주제는 결혼입니다. = Today's topic is marriage.

(Oh-neul joo-jeh-neun gyuhl-hoh-neeb-nee-dah.)

## marry

1. 결혼하다 (gyeolhonhada)

Sounds like "gyuhl-hohn-hah-dah"

ex. 결혼하셨어요? = Did you get married?

(Gyuhl-hohn-hah-shuh-ssuh-yoh?)

## mom

1. 엄마 (eomma)

Sounds like "uhm-mah"

ex. 엄마, 나 왔어. = Mom, I'm home.

(Uhm-mah, nah wah-ssuh.)

## mother

1. 어머니 (eomeoni)

Sounds like "uh-muh-nee"

ex. 오늘이 어머니 생신이세요. = Today is Mother's birthday.

(Oh-neu-ree uh-muh-nee saeng-shee-nee-seh-yoh.)

## name

1. 이름 (ireum), casual/informal form

Sounds like "ee-reum"

ex. 내 이름은 지현이야. = My name is Ji-hyeon.

(Nae ee-reu-meun jee-hyuh-nee-yah.)


2. 성함 (seongham), honorific/formal form

Sounds like "suhng-hahm"

ex. 성함이 어떻게 되십니까? = What is your name?

(Suhng-hah-mee uh-dduh-keh dweh-sheeb-nee-ggah?)


## neighbor

1. 이웃 (iut)

Sounds like "ee-woot"

ex. 이웃이 이사를 갔다. = The neighbor moved.

(Ee-woo-shee ee-sah-reul gaht-ddah.)


## parents

1. 부모님 (bumonim)

Sounds like "boo-moh-neem"

ex. 부모님은 안녕하시니? = How are your parents?

(Boo-moh-nee-meu nahn-nyuhng-hah-shee-nee?)

## person

1. 사람 (saram)

Sounds like "sah-rahm"

ex. 그 사람은 정말 못 됐다. = The person is really terrible.

(Geu sah-rah-meun juhng-mahl moht-ddwaet-ddah.)

## police

1. 경찰 (gyeongchal)

Sounds like "gyuhng-chahl"

ex. 경찰 좀 불러주세요. = Please call the police.

(Gyuhng-chahl johm bool-luh-joo-seh-yoh.)

## politician

1. 정치인 (jeongchiin)

Sounds like "juhng-chee-een"

ex. 정치인이 되는 게 꿈이다. = She wants to be a politician.

(Juhng-chee-ee-nee dweh-neun geh ggoo-mee-dah.)


## president

1. 대통령 (daetonglyeong)

Sounds like "dae-tohng-nyuhng"

ex. 어제 대통령을 만났다. = I met the President yesterday.

(Uh-jeh dae-tohng-nyuhng-eul mahn-naht-ddah.)

## queen

1. 여왕 (yeowang)

Sounds like "yuh-wahng"

ex. 여왕이 말을 하셨습니다. = The queen spoke.

(Yuh-wahng-ee mah-reul hah-shuht-sseub-nee-dah.)

## relative

1. 친척 (chincheok)

Sounds like "cheen-chuhg"

ex. 우리는 친척이야. = We are relatives.

(Woo-ree-neun cheen-chuh-ghee-yah.)

## security guard

1. 경비원 (gyeongbiwon)

Sounds like "gyuhng-bee-wuhn"

ex. 경비원한테 물어보세요. = Ask the security guard.

(Gyuhng-bee-wuhn-hahn-teh moo-ruh-boh-seh-yoh.)

## siblings

1. 형제자매 (hyeongjejamae)

Sounds like "hyuhng-jeh-jah-mae"

ex. 형제자매가 몇이야? = How many siblings do you have?

(Hyuhng-jeh-jah-mae-gah myuh-chee-yah?)

## sister

1. 언니 (eonni), woman's older sister or female friend

Sounds like "uhn-nee"

ex. 언니, 우리 영화 보자. = Sister, let's watch a movie.

(Uhn-nee, woo-ree yuhng-hwah boh-jah.)

2. 누나 (nuna), man's older sister or female friend

Sounds like "noo-nah"

ex. 누나랑 세 살 차이예요. = My sister is three years older.

(Noo-nah-rahng seh sahl chah-ee-yeah-yoh.)

3. 여동생 (yeodongsaeng), younger sister

Sounds like "yuh-dohng-saeng"

ex. 여동생은 미국에서 살아. = My sister lives in the U.S.

(Yuh-dohng-saeng-eun mee-goo-geh-suh sah-rah.)

### soldier

1. 군인 (gunin)

Sounds like "goo-neen"

ex. 여러 명의 군인이 뛰어가요. = Many soldiers are running.

(Yuh-ruh myuhng-eui goo-nee-nee ddwee-uh-gah-yoh.)

### son

1. 아들 (adeul)

Sounds like "ah-deul"

ex. 내 아들은 유학 중이야. = My son is studying abroad.

(Nae ah-deu-reu nyou-hahg jjoong-ee-yah.)

## teenager

1. 청소년 (cheongsonyeon)

Sounds like "chuhng-soh-nyuhn"

ex. 한 청소년이 인사를 했다. = A teenager said hello to me.

(Hahn chuhng-soh-nyuh-nee een-sah-reul haet-ddah.)

## transgender

1. 트랜스젠더 (teuraenseujendeo)

Sounds like "teu-raen-sseu-jehn-duh"

ex. 그녀는 트랜스젠더이다. = She is transgender.

(Geu-nyuh-neun teu-raen-sseu-jehn-duh-ee-dah.)

## twin

1. 쌍둥이 (ssangdungi)

Sounds like "ssahng-doong-ee"

ex. 얘네들은 쌍둥이예요. = They are twins.

(Ae-neh-deu-reun ssahng-doong-ee-yeah-yoh.)

## uncle

1. 삼촌 (samchon), father's unmarried younger brother

Sounds like "sahm-chohn"

ex. 그리고 이 분은 제 삼촌이세요. = And this is my uncle.

(Geu-ree-goh ee boo-neun jeh sahm-choh-nee-seh-yoh.)

2. 외삼촌 (wesamchon), mother's brother

Sounds like "weh-sahm-chohn"

ex. 외삼촌이 집으로 가셨다. = Uncle went home.

(Weh-sahm-choh-nee jee-beu-roh gah-shuht-ddah.)

3. 큰아버지 (keunabeoji), father's older brother

Sounds like "keu-nah-buh-jee"

ex. 다슬아, 큰아버지 오셨다. = Daseul, Uncle has arrived.

(Dah-seu-rah, keu-nah-buh-jee oh-shuht-ddah.)

4. 작은아버지 (jakeunabeoji), father's younger brother

Sounds like "jah-geu-nah-buh-jee"

ex. 작은아버지 불러와라. = Go and get your uncle.

(Jah-geu-nah-buh-jee bool-luh-wah-rah.)

5. 고모부 (gomobu), husband of father's sister

Sounds like "goh-moh-boo"

ex. 고모부랑 얘기를 나누었다. = I talked to Uncle.

(Goh-moh-boo-rahng ae-ghee-reul nah-noo-uht-ddah.)

6. 이모부 (imobu), husband of mother's sister

Sounds like "ee-moh-boo"

ex. 이모부께 인사 드려. = Say hello to your uncle.

(Ee-moh-boo-ggeh een-sah deu-ryuh.)

# white (people)

1. 백인 (baekin)

Sounds like "bae-gheen"

ex. 윌리엄스 씨가 백인인가요? = Is Mr. Williams white?

(Weel-lee-uhm-seu ssee-gah bae-ghee-neen-gah-yoh?)

# wife

1. 아내 (anae)

Sounds like "ah-nae"

ex. 내 아내는 일본 사람이다. = My wife is Japanese.

(Nae ah-nae-neu neel-bohn sah-rah-mee-dah.)

## woman

1. 여자 (yeoja)

Sounds like "yuh-jah"

ex. 여자들은 어디로 갔어요? = Where did the women go?

(Yuh-jah-deu-reu nuh-dee-roh gah-ssuh-yoh?)

# 3. Travel

## address

1. 주소 (juso)

Sounds like "joo-soh"

ex. 주소 좀 알려줘. = Tell me your address.

(Joo-soh joh mahl-lyuh-jwuh.)

## airline

1. 항공 (hanggong)

Sounds like "hahng-gohng"

ex. 숨바항공이 최고예요. = Soomba Airlines is the best.

(Soom-bah-hahng-gohng-ee chweh-goh-yeah-yoh.)

## airport

1. 공항 (gonghang)

Sounds like "gohng-hahng"

ex. 공항에서 만나요. = Let's meet at the airport.

(Gohng-hahng-eh-suh mahn-nah-yoh.)

## arrival

1. 도착 (dochak)

Sounds like "doh-chahg"

ex. 도착 시간은 4시입니다. = The arrival time is 4 o'clock.

(Doh-chahg ssee-gah-neun neh-shee-eeb-nee-dah.)

## arrive

1. 도착하다 (dochakhada)

Sounds like "doh-chah-kah-dah"

ex. 방금 도착했어요. = I just arrived.

(Bahng-geum doh-chah-kae-ssuh-yoh.)

## bridge

1. 다리 (dari)

Sounds like "dah-ree"

ex. 다리가 많이 있다. = There are many bridges.

(Dah-ree-gah mah-nee eet-ddah.)

## camera

1. 카메라 (kamera)

Sounds like "kah-meh-rah"

ex. 어제 카메라를 잃어버렸어. = Yesterday, I lost my camera.

(Uh-jeh kah-meh-rah-reu ree-ruh-buh-lyuh-ssuh.)

## capital city

1. 수도 (sudo)

Sounds like "soo-doh"

ex. 한국의 수도는 서울. = Seoul, the capital city of Korea.

(Hahn-goo-geui soo-doh-neun suh-wool.)

## city

1. 도시 (dosi)

Sounds like "doh-shee"

ex. 그들은 큰 도시를 좋아해요. = They like big cities.

(Geu-deu-reun keun doh-shee-reul joh-ah-hae-yoh.)

## departure

1. 출발 (chulbal)

Sounds like "chool-bahl"

ex. 출발 이후에 도착했다. = I arrived after departure.

(Chool-bah ree-hoo-eh doh-chah-kaet-ddah.)

## direction

1. 방향 (banghyang)

Sounds like "bahng-hyahng"

ex. 어느 방향으로 갔어? = Which direction did she take?

(Uh-neu bahng-hyahng-eu-roh gah-ssuh?)

## distance

1. 거리 (geori)

Sounds like "guh-ree"

ex. 거리가 너무 멀다. = The distance is too far.

(Guh-ree-gah nuh-moo muhl-dah.)

## east

1. 동쪽 (dongjjok)

Sounds like "dohng-jjohg"

ex. 해는 동쪽에서 뜬다. = The Sun rises from the east.

(Hae-neun dohng-jjoh-geh-suh ddeun-dah.)


## East, the

1. 동양 (dongyang)

Sounds like "dohng-yahng"

ex. 피터는 동양에서 왔어요. = Peter came from the East.

(Pee-tuh-neun dohng-yahng-eh-suh wah-ssuh-yoh.)

## embassy

1. 대사관 (daesagwan)

Sounds like "dae-sah-gwahn"

ex. 미 대사관을 못 찾겠어요. = I can't find the U.S. Embassy.

(Mee dae-sah-gwah-neul moht chaht-ggeh-ssuh-yoh.)

## flight attendant

1. 승무원 (seungmuwon)

Sounds like "seung-moo-wuhn"

ex. 승무원에게 물어보았다. = She asked the flight attendant.

(Seung-moo-wuh-neh-geh moo-ruh-boh-aht-ddah.)

## hotel

1. 호텔 (hotel)

Sounds like "hoh-tehl"

ex. 오늘은 호텔에서 잘 거야. = I will sleep at a hotel tonight.

(Oh-neu-reun hoh-teh-reh-suh jahl gguh-yah.)

## ID

1. 신분증 (shinbunjeung)

Sounds like "sheen-boon-jjeung"

ex. 신분증 좀 보여주세요. = Can I see your ID, please?

(Sheen-boon-jjeung jjohm boh-yuh-joo-seh-yoh.)

## immigrant

1. 이주민 (ijumin)

Sounds like "ee-joo-meen"

ex. 저는 이주민이 아닙니다. = I am not an immigrant.

(Juh-neu nee-joo-mee-nee ah-neeb-nee-dah.)

## map

1. 지도 (jido)

Sounds like "jee-doh"

ex. 지도 앱을 설치하고 싶어요. = I'd like to install a map app.

(Jee-doh ae-beul suhl-chee-hah-goh shee-puh-yoh.)

## metro

1. 지하철 (jihacheol)

Sounds like "jee-hah-chuhl"

ex. 지하철을 타고 갔다. = I took the metro to go there.

(Jee-hah-chuh-reul tah-goh gaht-ddah.)

## motel

1. 모텔 (motel), general form

Sounds like "moh-tehl"

ex. 모텔을 찾아봐. = Look for a motel.

(Moh-teh-reul chah-jah-bwah.)

2. 여관 (yeogwan), alternative form

Sounds like "yuh-gwahn"

ex. 그는 지금 여관에 있다. = He is at a motel right now.

(Geu-neun jee-geu myuh-gwah-neh eet-ddah.)

## north

1. 북쪽 (bukjjok)

Sounds like "boog-jjohg"

ex. 북쪽으로 가시면 됩니다. = Go north to find it.

(Boog-jjoh-geu-roh gah-shee-myuhn dweb-nee-dah.)

## passport

1. 여권 (yeogwon)

Sounds like "yuh-ggwuhn"

ex. 여권을 잃어버렸어요. = I lost my passport.

(Yuh-ggwuh-neu ree-ruh-buh-ryuh-ssuh-yoh.)

## pilot

1. 조종사 (jojongsa)

Sounds like "joh-johng-sah"

ex. 조종사가 늦게 도착했다. = The pilot arrived late.

(Joh-johng-sah-gah neut-ggeh doh-chah-kaet-ddah.)

## south

1. 남쪽 (namjjok)

Sounds like "nahm-jjohg"

ex. 남쪽에 비가 오고 있습니다. = It is raining in the south.

(Nahm-jjoh-geh bee-gah oh-goh ee-sseub-nee-dah.)

## tourist

1. 관광객 (gwangwanggaeg), general form

Sounds like "gwahn-gwahng-gaeg"

ex. 저희는 관광객이에요. = We are tourists.

(Juh-hee-neun gwahn-gwahng-gae-ghee-eh-yoh.)

2. 여행객 (yeohaenggaek), alternative form

Sounds like "yuh-haeng-gaeg"

ex. 여행객이 좀 늘었어요. = We get more tourists now.

(Yuh-haeng-gae-ghee johm neu-ruh-ssuh-yoh.)

## travel

1. 여행 (yeohaeng), noun

Sounds like "yuh-haeng"

ex. 시간 여행은 가능할까? = Will time travel be possible?

(Shee-gah nyuh-haeng-eun gah-neung-hahl-ggah?)

2. 여행 가다 (yeohaeng gada), verb

Sounds like "yuh-haeng gah-dah"

ex. 부산으로 여행 가자. = Let's travel to Busan.

(Boo-sah-neu-roh yuh-haeng gah-jah.)

## trip

1. 여행 (yeohaeng), travel

Sounds like "yuh-haeng"

ex. 여행 잘 다녀왔어? = How was your trip?

(Yuh-haeng jahl dah-nyuh-wah-ssuh?)


2. 관광 (gwangwang), sightseeing

Sounds like "gwahn-gwahng"

ex. 중국으로 관광을 갔어요. = She took a trip to China.

(Joong-goo-geu-roh gwahn-gwahng-eul gah-ssuh-yoh.)


## vacation

1. 휴가 (hyuga)

Sounds like "hyou-gah"

ex. 저 다음 주에 휴가 가요. = I go on vacation next week.

(Juh dah-eum jjoo-eh hyou-gah gah-yoh.)


## west

1. 서쪽 (seojjok)

Sounds like "suh-jjohg"

ex. 저쪽이 서쪽인가요? = Is that west?

(Juh-jjoh-ghee suh-jjoh-gheen-gah-yoh?)

## West, the

1. 서양 (seoyang)

Sounds like "suh-yahng"

ex. 그는 서양에서 유명하다. = He is famous in the West.

(Geu-neun suh-yahng-eh-suh you-myuhng-hah-dah.)

## world

1. 세계 (segye)

Sounds like "seh-gyeah"

ex. 세계 지도를 하나 샀다. = I bought a world map.

(Seh-gyeah jee-doh-reul hah-nah saht-ddah.)

# 4. Languages

## adjective

1. 형용사 (hyeongyongsa)

Sounds like "hyuhng-yohng-sah"

ex. '예쁘다'는 형용사이다. = 'Pretty' is an adjective.

('Yeah-bbeu-dah'-neun hyuhng-yohng-sah-ee-dah.)

## adverb

1. 부사 (busa)

Sounds like "boo-sah"

ex. 부사는 자주 쓰인다. = Adverbs are used often.

(Boo-sah-neun jah-joo sseu-een-dah.)

## alphabet

1. 문자 (munja)

Sounds like "moon-jjah"

ex. 한국어 문자가 뭐예요? = What is the Korean alphabet?

(Hahn-goo-guh moon-jjah-gah mwuh-yeah-yoh?)

# Chinese (language)

1. 중국어 (junggugeo)

Sounds like "joong-goo-guh"

ex. 중국어 할 줄 알아요 = I know how to speak Chinese.

(Joong-goo-guh hahl jjoo rah-rah-yoh.)

# definition

1. 정의 (jeongui)

Sounds like "juhng-eui"

ex. '정의'가 정의다. = 'Definition' is the definition.

('Juhng-eui'-gah juhng-eui-dah.)

## dictionary

1. 사전 (sajeon)

Sounds like "sah-juhn"

ex. 한국어 사전이 필요해요. = I need a Korean dictionary.

(Hahn-goo-guh sah-juh-nee pee-ryoh-hae-yoh.)

## English (language)

1. 영어 (yeongeo)

Sounds like "yuhng-uh"

ex. 저는 영어 못해요. = I can't speak English.

(Juh-neun yuhng-uh moh-tae-yoh.)

## foreign language

1. 외국어 (wegugeo)

Sounds like "weh-goo-guh"

ex. 내가 외국어로 말을 했다. = I spoke in a foreign language.

(Nae-gah weh-goo-guh-roh mah-reul haet-ddah.)

## French (language)

1. 프랑스어 (peurangseueo), general form

Sounds like "peu-rahng-sseu-uh"

ex. 프랑스어를 배웠어요. = I learned French.

(Peu-rahng-sseu-uh-reul bae-wuh-ssuh-yoh.)

2. 불어 (buleo), alternative form

Sounds like "boo-ruh"

ex. 그가 불어로 인사를 했다. = He said hello in French.

(Geu-gah boo-ruh-roh een-sah-reul haet-ddah.)

## grammar

1. 문법 (munbeop)

Sounds like "moon-bbuhb"

ex. 문법이 어려운 거 같아요. = I think grammar is hard.

(Moon-bbuh-bee uh-ryuh-woon guh gah-tah-yoh.)

## greeting

1. 인사 (insa)

Sounds like "een-sah"

ex. 인사를 잘못했다. = I used an improper greeting.

(Een-sah-reul jahl-moh-taet-ddah.)

## Hindi

1. 힌디어 (hindieo)

Sounds like "heen-dee-uh"

ex. 힌디어를 배우고 싶어요. = I'd like to learn Hindi.

(Heen-dee-uh-reul bae-woo-goh shee-puh-yoh.)

## Japanese (language)

1. 일본어 (ilboneo)

Sounds like "eel-boh-nuh"

ex. 일본어를 잘하시네요. = You speak Japanese well.

(Eel-boh-nuh-reul jahl-hah-shee-neh-yoh.)

## Korean (language)

1. 한국어 (hangugeo)

Sounds like "hahn-goo-guh"

ex. 나랑 같이 한국어 배우자. = Let's study Korean together.

(Nah-rahng gah-chee hahn-goo-guh bae-woo-jah.)

## language

1. 언어 (eoneo), language in general

Sounds like "uh-nuh"

ex. 어떤 언어를 하세요? = What languages do you speak?

(Uh-dduh nuh-nuh-reul hah-seh-yoh?)

2. 국어 (gukeo), number of languages/Korean language

Sounds like "goo-guh"

ex. 그는 3개 국어를 한다. = He speaks three languages.

(Geu-neun sahm-gae goo-guh-reul hahn-dah.)

## mean

1. 뜻하다 (tteutada), general form

Sounds like "ddeu-tah-dah"

ex. 이 단어는 뭐를 뜻하나요? = What does this word mean?

(Ee dah-nuh-neun mwuh-reul ddeu-tah-nah-yoh?)

2. 의미하다 (uimihada), alternative form

Sounds like "eui-mee-hah-dah"

ex. 뭐를 의미하는지 모르겠어. = I don't know what it means.

(Mwuh-reu reui-mee-hah-neun-jee moh-reu-geh-ssuh.)

## meaning

1. 뜻 (tteut), general form

Sounds like "ddeut"

ex. 이게 무슨 뜻이에요? = What is the meaning of this?

(Ee-geh moo-seun ddeu-shee-eh-yoh?)

2. 의미 (uimi), alternative form

Sounds like "eui-mee"

ex. 단어의 의미를 외워라. = Memorize the word's meaning.

(Dah-nuh-eui eui-mee-reu rweh-wuh-rah.)

## native

1. 네이티브 (neitibeu), someone from a specific place

Sounds like "neh-ee-tee-beu"

ex. 네이티브이신 줄 알았어요. = You speak well like a native.

(Neh-ee-tee-beu-ee-sheen joo rah-rah-ssuh-yoh.)

2. 원어민 (wonamin), someone who is a native speaker

Sounds like "wuh-nuh-meen"

ex. 아뇨, 전 원어민이 아닙니다. = No, I am not a native.

(Ah-nyoh, juh nwuh-nuh-mee-nee ah-neeb-nee-dah.)

## paragraph

1. 문단 (mundan)

Sounds like "moon-dahn"

ex. 너가 문단을 읽어 보렴. = You can read the paragraph.

(Nuh-gah moon-dah-neu reel-guh boh-ryuhm.)

## parts of speech

1. 품사 (pumsa)

Sounds like "poom-sah"

ex. 이 품사를 설명해 주세요. = Explain this part of speech.

(Ee poom-sah-reul suhl-myuhng-hae joo-seh-yoh.)

## phrase

1. 관용구 (gwanyonggu)

Sounds like "gwah-nyohng-ggoo"

ex. 오늘 관용구를 배웠다. = I learned about phrases today.

(Oh-neul gwah-nyohng-ggoo-reul bae-wuht-ddah.)

# pronounce

1. 발음하다 (bareumhada)

Sounds like "bah-reum-hah-dah"

ex. 이거는 어떻게 발음해요? = How do I pronounce this?

(Ee-guh-neu nuh-dduh-keh bah-reum-hae-yoh?)

# pronunciation

1. 발음 (bareum)

Sounds like "bah-reum"

ex. 발음 연습을 하고 있어요. = I'm practicing pronunciation.

(Bah-reu myuhn-seu-beul hah-goh ee-ssuh-yoh.)

## Russian (language)

1. 러시아어 (reosiaeo)

Sounds like "ruh-shee-ah-uh"

ex. 러시아어를 조금 알아. = I know Russian a little bit.

(Ruh-shee-ah-uh-reul joh-geu mah-rah.)


## sentence

1. 문장 (munjang)

Sounds like "moon-jahng"

ex. 문장이 너무 어려워요. = This sentence is too difficult.

(Moon-jahng-ee nuh-moo uh-ryuh-wuh-yoh.)


## sound

1. 소리 (sori), noun

Sounds like "soh-ree"

ex. 소리가 아름답다. = The sound is beautiful.

(Soh-ree-gah ah-reum-dahb-ddah.)


2. 소리가 나다 (soriga nada), verb

Sounds like "soh-ree-gah nah-dah"

ex. 정말 비슷한 소리가 나네요. = It really sounds similar.

(Juhng-mahl bee-seu-tahn soh-ree-gah nah-neh-yoh.)

## Spanish (language)

1. 스페인어 (seupeineo)

Sounds like "seu-peh-ee-nuh"

ex. 스페인어는 어려운가요? = Is the Spanish language hard?

(Seu-peh-ee-nuh-neu nuh-ryuh-woon-gah-yoh?)

## speak

1. 말하다 (malhada), say something out loud

Sounds like "mahl-hah-dah"

ex. 이제 네가 말할 차례야. = Now it's your turn to speak.

(Ee-jeh neh-gah mahl-hahl chah-ryeah-yah.)

2. 할 줄 알다 (hal jul alda), speak a language

Sounds like "hahl jjool ahl-dah"

ex. 광둥어 할 줄 아세요? = Can you speak Cantonese?

(Gwahng-doong-uh hahl jjoo rah-seh-yoh?)

## spell

1. 쓰다 (sseuda)

Sounds like "sseu-dah"

ex. '코리아'는 어떻게 쓰나요? = How do you spell 'Korea?'

('Koh-ree-ah'-neu nuh-dduh-keh sseu-nah-yoh?)

## spelling

1. 스펠링 (seupelling), used for English words

Sounds like "seu-pehl-ling"

ex. 스펠링이 틀렸다. = The spelling is wrong.

(Seu-pehl-ling-ee teul-lyut-ddah.)

2. 맞춤법 (matchumbeop), used for Korean words

Sounds like "maht-choom-bbuhb"

ex. 맞춤법 검사 할래요. = I want to check for spelling errors.

(Maht-choom-bbuhb guhm-sah hahl-lae-yoh.)

## translate

1. 번역하다 (beonyeokada), translate written words

Sounds like "buh-nyuh-kah-dah"

ex. 구글 번역으로 번역해. = Translate with Google Translate.

(Goo-geul buh-nyuh-geu-roh buh-nyuh-kae.)

2. 통역하다 (tongyeokada), interpret languages

Sounds like "tohng-yuh-kah-dah"

ex. 내가 통역해 줄게. = I will translate for you.

(Nae-gah tohng-yuh-kae jool-ggeh.)

## translator

1. 번역가 (beonyeokga), text translator

Sounds like "buh-nyuhg-ggah"

ex. 저는 번역가 일을 합니다. = I work as a translator.

(Juh-neun buh-nyuhg-ggah ee-reul hahb-nee-dah.)

2. 통역사 (tongyeoksa), interpreter

Sounds like "tohng-yuhg-ssah"

ex. 통역사가 필요할 거 같아요. = I think we need a translator.

(Tohng-yuhg-ssah-gah pee-ryoh-hahl gguh gah-tah-yoh.)

## vocabulary

1. 어휘 (eohwi)

Sounds like "uh-hwee"

ex. 오늘 어휘 시험이 있어. = I have a vocabulary test today.

(Oh-neu ruh-hwee shee-huh-mee ee-ssuh.)

## voice

1. 목소리 (moksori)

Sounds like "mohg-ssoh-ree"

ex. 목소리가 마음에 들어요. = I like your voice.

(Mohg-ssoh-ree-gah mah-eu-meh deu-ruh-yoh.)

## word

1. 단어 (daneo)

Sounds like "dah-nuh"

ex. 단어가 언어를 만든다. = Words make up languages.

(Dah-nuh-gah uh-nuh-reul mahn-deun-dah.)

# 5. Things

### appliance

1. 기기 (gigi)

Sounds like "ghee-ghee"

ex. 기기가 고장 났다. = The appliance got broken.

(Ghee-ghee-gah goh-jahng naht-ddah.)

### bag

1. 가방 (gabang), bag made of fabric or leather

Sounds like "gah-bahng"

ex. 가방이 더 필요해요. = We need more bags.

(Gah-bahng-ee duh pee-ryoh-hae-yoh.)

2. 봉지 (bongji), bag made of paper or plastic

Sounds like "bohng-jee"

ex. 봉지 필요하세요? = Would you like a plastic bag?

(Bohng-jee pee-ryoh-hah-seh-yoh?)

3. 백 (baek), purse/handbag

Sounds like "bbaeg"

ex. 백 사러 가자. = Let's go buy a bag.

(Bbaeg sah-ruh gah-jah.)

## bicycle

1. 자전거 (jajeongeo)

Sounds like "jah-juhn-guh"

ex. 이 자전거는 비싼 거예요. = This is an expensive bicycle.

(Ee ja-juhn-guh-neun bee-ssahn guh-yeah-yoh.)

## boat

1. 배 (bae)

Sounds like "bae"

ex. 나는 배 타면 멀미해. = I get seasick when I'm on a boat.

(Nah-neun bae tah-myuhn muhl-mee-hae.)

## box

1. 상자 (sangja), alternative form

Sounds like "sahng-jah"

ex. 접시를 상자에 담아. = Put the dishes in the box.

(Juhb-ssee-reul sahng-jah-eh dah-mah.)

2. 박스 (bakseu), general form

Sounds like "bbahg-sseu"

ex. 고양이가 박스 안에 있네요. = The cat is inside the box.

(Goh-yahng-ee-gah bbahg-sseu ah-neh eet-neh-yoh.)

## comic book

1. 만화책 (manhwachaek)

Sounds like "mahn-hwah-chaeg"

ex. 나 만화책 좀 빌려줘. = Can I borrow your comic book?

(Nah mahn-hwah-chaeg jjohm beel-lyuh-jwuh.)

## doll

1. 인형 (inhyeong)

Sounds like "een-hyuhng"

ex. 저 인형은 얼마예요? = How much is that doll?

(Juh een-hyuhng-eu nuhl-mah-yeah-yoh?)


## fan

1. 선풍기 (seonpunggi)

Sounds like "suhn-poong-ghee"

ex. 선풍기 켜 봐. = Turn on the fan.

(Suhn-poong-ghee kyuh bwah.)


## glasses

1. 안경 (angyeong)

Sounds like "ahn-gyuhng"

ex. 안경이 안 보여요. = I can't find my glasses.

(Ahn-gyuhng-ee ahn boh-yuh-yoh.)

## gun

1. 총 (chong)

Sounds like "chong"

ex. 총을 가지고 계십니까? = Do you have a gun?

(Chohng-eul gah-jee-goh gyeah-sheeb-nee-ggah?)


## magazine

1. 잡지 (japji)

Sounds like "jahb-jjee"

ex. 잡지 하나만요. = One magazine, please.

(Jahb-jjee hah-nah-mahn-yoh.)

## motorcycle

1. 오토바이 (otobai)

Sounds like "oh-toh-bah-ee"

ex. 난 오토바이 타 봤어. = I've ridden a motorcycle before.

(Nah noh-toh-bah-ee tah bwah-ssuh.)

## newspaper

1. 신문 (shinmun)

Sounds like "sheen-moon"

ex. 아빠가 신문을 보신다. = Dad is reading the newspaper.

(Ah-bbah-gah sheen-moo-neul boh-sheen-dah.)

## object

1. 물체 (mulche)

Sounds like "mool-cheh"

ex. 이 물체는 이상해요. = This object is weird.

(Ee mool-cheh-neu nee-sahng-hae-yoh.)

## part

1. 부분 (bubun)

Sounds like "boo-boon"

ex. 이 부분은 뭐지? = What is this part?

(Ee boo-boo-neun mwuh-jee?)

## radio

1. 라디오 (radio)

Sounds like "rah-dee-oh"

ex. 오늘 라디오를 들었습니다. = I listened to the radio today.

(Oh-neul rah-dee-oh-reul deu-ruht-sseub-nee-dah.)

## scissors

1. 가위 (gawi)

Sounds like "gah-wee"

ex. 가위 좀 빌려주세요. = Can I borrow a pair of scissors?

(Gah-wee johm beel-lyuh-joo-seh-yoh.)

# thing

1. 물건 (mulgeon)

Sounds like "mool-guhn"

ex. 저건 무슨 물건이야? = What is that thing?

(Juh-guhn moo-seun mool-guh-nee-yah?)

# toy

1. 장난감 (jangnangam), general form

Sounds like "jahng-nahn-ggahm"

ex. 조카한테 장난감을 줬다. = I gave a toy to my nephew.

(Joh-kah-hahn-teh jahng-nahn-ggah-meul jwuht-ddah.)

2. 토이 (toi), alternative form

Sounds like "toh-ee"

ex. 가서 토이 갖고 놀아. = Go and play with your toys.

(Gah-suh toh-ee gaht-ggoh noh-rah.)

## umbrella

1. 우산 (usan)

Sounds like "woo-sahn"

ex. 혹시 우산 파시나요? = Do you happen to sell umbrellas?

(Hohg-ssee woo-sahn pah-shee-nah-yoh?)

## watch (thing)

1. 시계 (shigye)

Sounds like "shee-gyeah"

ex. 선물로 받은 시계야. = I got this watch as a gift.

(Suhn-mool-loh bah-deun shee-gyeah-yah.)

# 6. Auto

## auto

1. 차 (cha)

Sounds like "chah"

ex. 차 잡지를 읽고 있어. = I'm reading an auto magazine.

(Chah jahb-jjee-reu reel-ggoh ee-ssuh.)

## auto insurance

1. 자동차 보험 (jadongcha boheom)

Sounds like "jah-dohng-chah boh-huhm"

ex. 자동차 보험 없어요. = I don't have an auto insurance.

(Jah-dohng-chah boh-huh muhb-ssuh-yoh.)

## auto mechanic (place)

1. 자동차 정비소 (jadongcha jeongbiso)

Sounds like "jah-dohng-chah juhng-bee-soh"

ex. 자동차 정비소가 어디야? = Where is the auto mechanic?

(Jah-dohng-chah juhng-bee-soh-gah uh-dee-yah?)

## automobile

1. 자동차 (jadongcha)

Sounds like "jah-dohng-chah"

ex. 자동차 공장에서 일해. = I work at an automobile factory.

(Jah-dohng-chah gohng-jahng-eh-suh eel-hae.)

## car

1. 차 (cha), car in general

Sounds like "chah"

ex. 차 타고 왔어. = I came by car.

(Chah tah-goh wah-ssuh.)

2. 승용차 (seungyongcha), sedan

Sounds like "seung-yohng-chah"

ex. 승용차를 새로 샀다. = I bought a new car.

(Seung-yohng-chah-reul sae-roh saht-ddah.)

## car accident

1. 자동차 사고 (jadongcha sago)

Sounds like "jah-dohng-chah sah-goh"

ex. 자동차 사고가 났어요. = There was a car accident.

(Jah-dohng-chah sah-goh-gah nah-ssuh-yoh.)

## crosswalk

1. 횡단보도 (hoengdanbodo), general form

Sounds like "hwehng-dahn-boh-doh"

ex. 횡단보도를 건너와. = Cross the crosswalk toward me.

(Hwehng-dahn-boh-doh-reul guhn-nuh-wah.)

2. 건널목 (geonneolmok), alternative form

Sounds like "guhn-nuhl-mohg"

ex. 건널목에서 기다릴게. = I'll wait for you at the crosswalk.

(Guhn-nuhl-moh-geh-suh ghee-dah-reel-ggeh.)

## diesel

1. 디젤 (dijel)

Sounds like "dee-jehl"

ex. 이 차는 디젤이에요. = This car is diesel.

(Ee chah-neun dee-jeh-ree-eh-yoh.)

## drive

1. 운전하다 (unjeonhada)

Sounds like "woon-juhn-hah-dah"

ex. 운전할 줄 아세요? = Do you know how to drive?

(Woon-juhn-hahl jjoo rah-seh-yoh?)

## driver

1. 운전사 (unjeonsa)

Sounds like "woon-juhn-sah"

ex. 버스 운전사가 말했다. = The bus driver spoke.

(Buh-sseu woon-juhn-sah-gah mahl-haet-ddah.)

## driver's license

1. 운전면허증 (unjeonmyeonheojeung)

Sounds like "woon-juhn-myuhn-huh-jjeung"

ex. 운전면허증 좀 보여 줘. = Show me your driver's license.

(Woon-juhn-myuhn-huh-jjeung johm boh-yuh jwuh.)

## gas station

1. 주유소 (juyuso)

Sounds like "joo-you-soh"

ex. 주유소가 어디 있나요? = Where is the gas station?

(Joo-you-soh-gah uh-dee eet-nah-yoh?)

## gasoline

1. 휘발유 (hwibalyu), general form

Sounds like "hwee-bahl-lyou"

ex. 휘발유 가격이 올랐다. = The gasoline price has gone up.

(Hwee-bahl-lyou gah-gyuh-ghee ohl-laht-ddah.)

2. 가솔린 (gasollin), alternative form

Sounds like "gah-sohl-leen"

ex. 이 차는 가솔린 차입니까? = Is this a gasoline car?

(Ee chah-neun gah-sohl-leen chah-eeb-nee-ggah?)

## GPS system

1. 내비게이션 (naebigeisyeon)

Sounds like "nae-bee-geh-ee-shuhn"

ex. 내비게이션을 달았어. = I installed a GPS system.

(Nae-bee-geh-ee-shuh-neul dah-rah-ssuh.)

## highway

1. 고속 도로 (gosok doro)

Sounds like "goh-sohg ddoh-roh"

ex. 고속 도로가 막힌다. = The highway is jammed with cars.

(Goh-sohg ddoh-roh-gah mah-keen-dah.)

## hood (auto)

1. 본네트 (bonneteu)

Sounds like "bohn-neh-teu"

ex. 본네트를 어떻게 열어요? = How do I open the hood?

(Bohn-neh-teu-reu ruh-dduh-keh yuh-ruh-yoh?)

## insurance

1. 보험 (boheom)

Sounds like "boh-huhm"

ex. 보험에 드셨나요? = Do you have insurance?

(Boh-huh-meh deu-shuht-nah-yoh?)

## lane (auto)

1. 차선 (chaseon)

Sounds like "chah-suhn"

ex. 일 차선으로 옮겨. = Switch to the first lane.

(Eel chah-suh-neu-roh ohm-gyuh.)

## park (auto)

1. 주차하다 (juchahada)

Sounds like "joo-chah-hah-dah"

ex. 주차할 곳이 없다. = There is no place to park.

(Joo-chah-hahl ggoh-shee uhb-ddah.)

## ride

1. 타다 (tada)

Sounds like "tah-dah"

ex. 택시 타고 있어. = I'm riding a taxi.

(Taeg-ssee tah-goh ee-ssuh.)

## road

1. 도로 (doro)

Sounds like "doh-roh"

ex. 왜 도로를 건너가니? = Why are you crossing the road?

(Wae doh-roh-reul guhn-nuh-gah-nee?)

# road sign

1. 표지판 (pyojipan)

Sounds like "pyoh-jee-pahn"

ex. 표지판에 영어로 써있어요. = English is on road signs.

(Pyoh-jee-pah-neh yuhng-uh-roh ssuh-ee-ssuh-yoh.)

# seat

1. 좌석 (jwaseok)

Sounds like "jwah-suhg"

ex. 빈 좌석이 없잖아! = There are no empty seats!

(Been jwah-suh-ghee uhb-jjah-nah!)

# seatbelt

1. 안전벨트 (anjeonbelteu)

Sounds like "ahn-juhn-behl-teu"

ex. 안전벨트를 착용하세요. = Please put on your seatbelt.

(Ahn-juhn-behl-teu-reul chah-gyohng-hah-seh-yoh.)

## speed

1. 속도 (sokdo)

Sounds like "sohg-ddoh"

ex. KTX 속도는 빠르다. = The speed of KTX trains is fast.

(Keh-ee-tee-ehg-sseu sohg-ddoh-neun bbah-reu-dah.)

## speed limit

1. 제한 속도 (jehan sokdo)

Sounds like "jeh-hahn sohg-ddoh"

ex. 제한 속도가 어떻게 되나요? = What is the speed limit?

(Jeh-hahn sohg-ddoh-gah uh-dduh-keh dweh-nah-yoh?)


## tire

1. 타이어 (taieo)

Sounds like "tah-ee-uh"

ex. 타이어에 구멍이 났다. = The tire went flat.

(Tah-ee-uh-eh goo-muhng-ee naht-ddah.)

## traffic

1. 교통 혼잡 (gyotong honjap)

Sounds like "gyoh-tohng hohn-jahb"

ex. 서울은 교통 혼잡이 심해. = Traffic in Seoul is terrible.

(Suh-woo-reun gyoh-tohng hohn-jah-bee sheem-hae.)

## traffic light

1. 신호등 (shinhodeung)

Sounds like "sheen-hoh-deung"

ex. 신호등 불이 바뀌었다. = The traffic light changed color.

(Sheen-hoh-deung bboo-ree bah-ggwee-uht-ddah.)

## truck

1. 트럭 (teureok)

Sounds like "teu-ruhg"

ex. 저는 트럭 운전사입니다. = I am a truck driver.

(Juh-neun teu-ruh gwoon-juhn-sah-eeb-nee-dah.)

## trunk

1. 트렁크 (teureongkeu)

Sounds like "teu-ruhng-keu"

ex. 짐을 트렁크에 실어요. = Put the load in the trunk.

(Jee-meul teu-ruhng-keu-eh shee-ruh-yoh.)

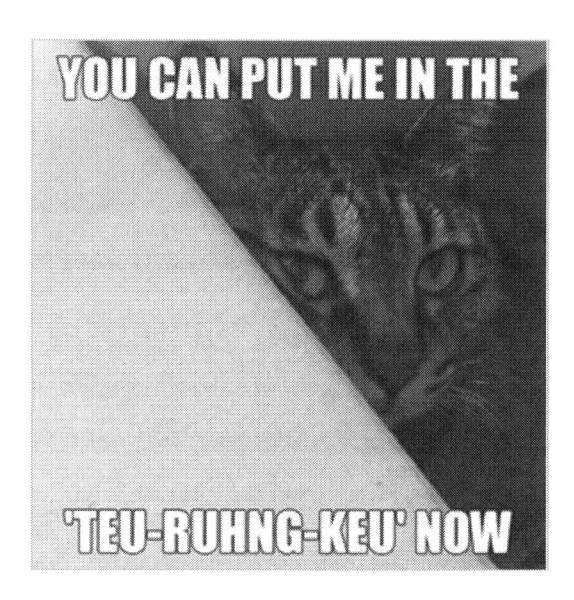

## van

1. 밴 (baen)

Sounds like "baen"

ex. 저건 학원 밴이야. = That's a tutoring-center van.

(Juh-guhn hah-gwuhn bae-nee-yah.)

## way (auto)

1. 길 (gil)

Sounds like "gheel"

ex. 어떤 길로 가야죠? = Which way should I take?

(Uh-dduhn gheel-loh gah-yah-jyoh?)

## wheel

1. 운전대 (unjeondae), general form of steering wheel

Sounds like "woon-juhn-ddae"

ex. 운전대를 잡으면 안 돼. = You should not grab the wheel.

(Woon-juhn-ddae-reul jah-beu-myuh nahn dwae.)

2. 핸들 (haendeul), alternative form of steering wheel

Sounds like "haen-deul"

ex. 핸들을 왼쪽으로 꺾으세요. = Turn the wheel to the left.

(Haen-deu-reu rwehn-jjoh-geu-roh gguh-ggeu-seh-yoh.)

3. 바퀴 (bakwi), as in "wagon wheel"

Sounds like "bah-kwee"

ex. 바퀴가 빠졌다. = A wheel came off.

(Bah-kwee-gah bbah-juht-ddah.)

# 7. Hospitals & Pharmacies

## ambulance

1. 구급차 (gugeupcha), general form

Sounds like "goo-geub-chah"

ex. 구급차가 오고 있다. = An ambulance is coming.

(Goo-geub-chah-gah oh-goh eet-ddah.)


2. 앰뷸런스 (aembyulleonseu), alternative form

Sounds like "aem-byoul-luhn-sseu"

ex. 앰뷸런스를 불러 주세요. = Please call an ambulance.

(Aem-byoul-luhn-sseu-reul bool-luh joo-seh-yoh.)


## dentist

1. 치과 (chigwa), dental hospital

Sounds like "chee-ggwah"

ex. 치과에 다녀왔어. = I went to the dentist.

(Chee-ggwah-eh dah-nyuh-wah-ssuh.)

2. 치과 의사 (chigwa uisa), doctor of dentistry

Sounds like "chee-ggwah eui-sah"

ex. 치과 의사가 여러 명이다. = There are many dentists.

(Chee-ggwah eui-sah-gah yuh-ruh myuhng-ee-dah.)

## doctor

1. 의사 (uisa)

Sounds like "eui-sah"

ex. 의사 선생님, 저 민지예요. = Doctor, it's Minzy.

(Eui-sah suhn-saeng-neem, juh meen-jee-yeah-yoh.)

## drug

1. 약 (yak), pill/medicine

Sounds like "yahg"

ex. 약 좀 먹어야겠어. = I think I need to take a drug.

(Yahg jjohm muh-guh-yah-geh-ssuh.)


2. 마약 (mayak), narcotics

Sounds like "mah-yahg"

ex. 마약을 사다가 걸렸다. = He got caught buying drugs.

(Mah-yah-geul sah-dah-gah guhl-lyuht-ddah.)


## emergency

1. 응급 상황 (eunggeup sanghwang)

Sounds like "eung-geub sahng-hwahng"

ex. 응급 상황이에요. = It's an emergency.

(Eung-geub sahng-hwahng-ee-eh-yoh.)


## hospital

1. 병원 (byeongwon)

Sounds like "byuhng-wuhn"

ex. 그가 병원에 입원하였다. = He checked into a hospital.

(Geu-gah byuhng-wuh-neh ee-bwuhn-hah-yuht-ddah.)

## medical condition

1. 질환 (jilhwan)

Sounds like "jeel-hwahn"

ex. 저는 질환이 있어요. = I have a medical condition.

(Juh-neun jeel-hwah-nee ee-ssuh-yoh.)

## medicine

1. 약 (yak)

Sounds like "yahg"

ex. 모르는 게 약이다. = Ignorance is the best medicine.

(Moh-reu-neun geh yah-ghee-dah.)

## nurse

1. 간호사 (ganhosa)

Sounds like "gahn-hoh-sah"

ex. 간호사 어디 갔어요? = Where did the nurse go?

(Gahng-hoh-sah uh-dee gah-ssuh-yoh?)

## pharmacist

1. 약사 (yaksa)

Sounds like "yahg-ssah"

ex. 아마 약사가 알 거예요. = I'm sure the pharmacist knows.

(Ah-mah yahg-ssah-gah ahl gguh-yeah-yoh.)

## pharmacy

1. 약국 (yakguk)

Sounds like "yahg-ggoog"

ex. 약국이 어디에 있습니까? = Where is the pharmacy?

(Yahg-ggoo-ghee uh-dee-eh eet-sseub-nee-ggah?)

## pill

1. 알약 (alyak)

Sounds like "ahl-lyahg"

ex. 알약을 먹어야 해. = I need to take a pill.

(Ahl-lyah-geul muh-guh-yah hae.)

## prescription

1. 처방전 (cheobangjeon)

Sounds like "chuh-bahng-juhn"

ex. 처방전이 있어야 됩니다. = You need a prescription.

(Chuh-bahng-juh-nee ee-ssuh-yah dweb-nee-dah.)

# Ch. 1 Self Quiz

he

I

pronoun

she

that

there

these

they

this

those

we

you

# Ch. 1 Answers

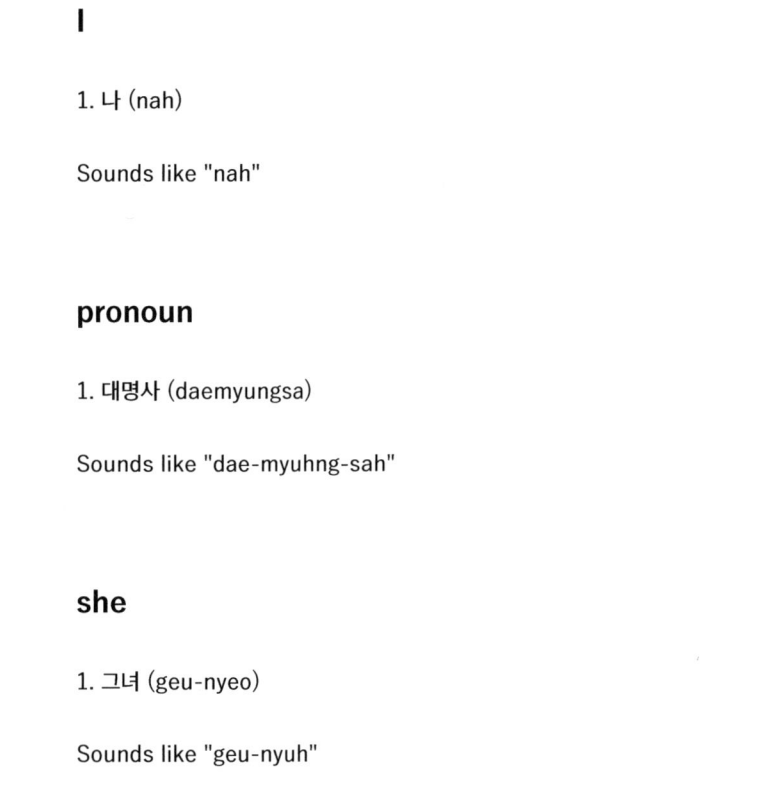

**he**

1. 그 (geu)

Sounds like "geu"

**I**

1. 나 (nah)

Sounds like "nah"

**pronoun**

1. 대명사 (daemyungsa)

Sounds like "dae-myuhng-sah"

**she**

1. 그녀 (geu-nyeo)

Sounds like "geu-nyuh"

## that

1. 저 (jeo), as in "that person"

Sounds like "juh"


2. 저것 (jeogeot), as in "that means"

Sounds like "juh-guht"


## there

1. 저기 (jeogi)

Sounds like "juh-ghee"


## these

1. 이것들 (igeotdeul)

Sounds like "ee-guh-ddeul"


## they

1. 그들 (geudeul)

Sounds like "geu-deul"

## this

1. 이 (i), as in "this pencil"

Sounds like "ee"

2. 이것 (igeot), as in "this is"

Sounds like "ee-guht"

## those

1. 저것들 (jeogeotdeul)

Sounds like "juh-guht-ddeul"

## we

1. 우리 (wuri)

Sounds like "woo-ree"

## you

1. 너 (neo), informal/casual form

Sounds like "nuh"

2. 당신 (dangshin), formal/honorific form

Sounds like "dahng-sheen"

# Ch. 2 Self Quiz

adult

age

Asian

aunt

baby

barber

black (people)

boy

brother

child

citizen

cop

cousin

dad

daughter

father

female, the

firefighter

first name

foreigner

friend

gender

girl

granddaughter

grandparents

grandson

human

husband

kid

king

last name

male, the

man

marriage

marry

mom

mother

name

neighbor

parents

person

police

politician

president

queen

relative

security guard

siblings

sister

soldier

son

teenager

transgender

twin

uncle

white (people)

wife

woman

# Ch. 2 Answers

### adult

1. 성인 (seongin)

Sounds like "suhng-een"

### age

1. 나이 (nai)

Sounds like "nah-ee"

### Asian

1. 아시아인 (asiain)

Sounds like "ah-shee-ah-een"

### aunt

1. 큰어머니 (keuneomeoni), wife of father's older brother

Sounds like "keu-nuh-muh-nee"

2. 작은어머니 (jakeuneomeoni), wife of dad's younger bro.

Sounds like "jah-geu-nuh-muh-nee"

3. 고모 (gomo), sister of one's father

Sounds like "goh-moh"

4. 이모 (imo), sister of one's mother

Sounds like "ee-moh"

5. 외숙모 (wesukmo), wife of brother of one's mother

Sounds like "weh-soong-moh"

## baby

1. 아기 (agi), human baby

Sounds like "ah-ghee"

2. 새끼 (saeggi), animal baby

Sounds like "sae-gghee"

## barber

1. 이발사 (ibalsa)

Sounds like "ee-bahl-ssah"

## black (people)

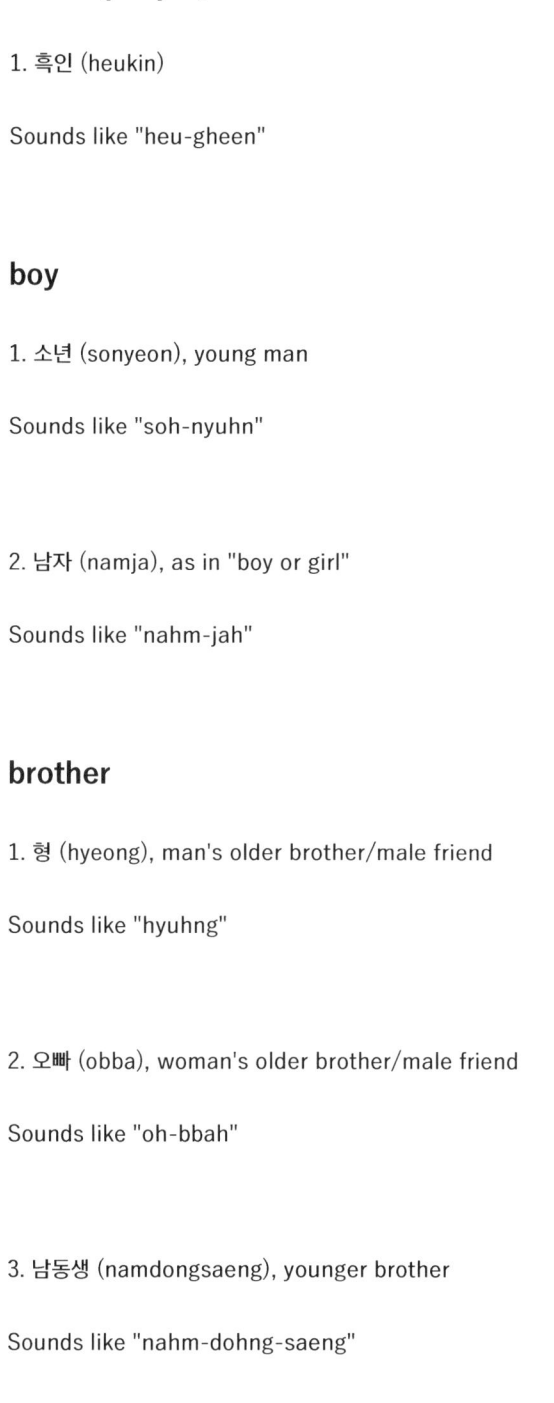

1. 흑인 (heukin)

Sounds like "heu-gheen"

## boy

1. 소년 (sonyeon), young man

Sounds like "soh-nyuhn"

2. 남자 (namja), as in "boy or girl"

Sounds like "nahm-jah"

## brother

1. 형 (hyeong), man's older brother/male friend

Sounds like "hyuhng"

2. 오빠 (obba), woman's older brother/male friend

Sounds like "oh-bbah"

3. 남동생 (namdongsaeng), younger brother

Sounds like "nahm-dohng-saeng"

## child

1. 어린이 (eorini), very young person

Sounds like "uh-reen-ee"

2. 아이 (ai), kid or one's own kid

Sounds like "ah-ee"

## citizen

1. 국민 (gukmin)

Sounds like "goong-meen"

## cop

1. 경찰 (gyeongchal)

Sounds like "gyuhng-chahl"

## cousin

1. 사촌 (sachon)

Sounds like "sah-chohn"

## dad

1. 아빠 (abba)

Sounds like "ah-bbah"

## daughter

1. 딸 (ttal)

Sounds like "ddahl"

## father

1. 아버지 (abeoji)

Sounds like "ah-buh-jee"

## female, the

1. 여성 (yeoseong)

Sounds like "yuh-suhng"

## firefighter

1. 소방관 (sobanggwan)

Sounds like "soh-bahng-gwahn"

## first name

1. 이름 (ireum)

Sounds like "ee-reum"

## foreigner

1. 외국인 (wegukin)

Sounds like "weh-goo-gheen"

## friend

1. 친구 (chingu)

Sounds like "cheen-goo"

## gender

1. 성 (seong)

Sounds like "suhng"

## girl

1. 소녀 (sonyeo), young woman

Sounds like "soh-nyuh"

2. 여자 (yeoja), as in "boy or girl"

Sounds like "yuh-jah"

## granddaughter

1. 손녀 (sonnyeo)

Sounds like "sohn-nyuh"

## grandparents

1. 할아버지 할머니 (halabeoji halmeoni)

Sounds like "hah-rah-buh-jee hahl-muh-nee"

## grandson

1. 손자 (sonja)

Sounds like "sohn-jah"

## human

1. 인간 (ingan)

Sounds like "een-gahn"

## husband

1. 남편 (nampyeon)

Sounds like "nahm-pyuhn"

## kid

1. 애 (ae), person not fully grown up or matured

Sounds like "ae"

2. 아이 (ai), child or my child

Sounds like "ah-ee"

## king

1. 왕 (wang)

Sounds like "wahng"

## last name

1. 성 (seong)

Sounds like "suhng"

## male, the

1. 남성 (namseong)

Sounds like "nahm-suhng"

## man

1. 남자 (namja)

Sounds like "nahm-jah"

## marriage

1. 결혼 (gyeolhon)

Sounds like "gyuhl-hohn"

## marry

1. 결혼하다 (gyeolhonhada)

Sounds like "gyuhl-hohn-hah-dah"

## mom

1. 엄마 (eomma)

Sounds like "uhm-mah"

## mother

1. 어머니 (eomeoni)

Sounds like "uh-muh-nee"

## name

1. 이름 (ireum), casual/informal form

Sounds like "ee-reum"

2. 성함 (seongham), honorific/formal form

Sounds like "suhng-hahm"

## neighbor

1. 이웃 (iut)

Sounds like "ee-woot"

## parents

1. 부모님 (bumonim)

Sounds like "boo-moh-neem"

## person

1. 사람 (saram)

Sounds like "sah-rahm"

## police

1. 경찰 (gyeongchal)

Sounds like "gyuhng-chahl"

## politician

1. 정치인 (jeongchiin)

Sounds like "juhng-chee-een"

## president

1. 대통령 (dactonglyeong)

Sounds like "dae-tohng-nyuhng"

## queen

1. 여왕 (yeowang)

Sounds like "yuh-wahng"

## relative

1. 친척 (chincheok)

Sounds like "cheen-chuhg"

## security guard

1. 경비원 (gyeongbiwon)

Sounds like "gyuhng-bee-wuhn"

## siblings

1. 형제자매 (hyeongjejamae)

Sounds like "hyuhng-jeh-jah-mae"

## sister

1. 언니 (eonni), woman's older sister/female friend

Sounds like "uhn-nee"

2. 누나 (nuna), man's older sister/female friend

Sounds like "noo-nah"

3. 여동생 (yeodongsaeng), younger sister

Sounds like "yuh-dohng-saeng"

## soldier

1. 군인 (gunin)

Sounds like "goo-neen"

## son

1. 아들 (adeul)

Sounds like "ah-deul"

## teenager

1. 청소년 (cheongsonyeon)

Sounds like "chuhng-soh-nyuhn"

## transgender

1. 트랜스젠더 (teuraenseujendeo)

Sounds like "teu-raen-sseu-jehn-duh"

## twin

1. 쌍둥이 (ssangdungi)

Sounds like "ssahng-doong-ee"

## uncle

1. 삼촌 (samchon), unmarried brother of one's father

Sounds like "sahm-chohn"

2. 외삼촌 (wesamchon), brother of one's mother

Sounds like "weh-sahm-chohn"

3. 큰아버지 (keunabeoji), older brother of one's father

Sounds like "keu-nah-buh-jee"

4. 작은아버지 (jakeunabeoji), father's married younger bro.

Sounds like "jah-geu-nah-buh-jee"

5. 고모부 (gomobu), husband of one's father-side aunt

Sounds like "goh-moh-boo"

6. 이모부 (imobu), husband of one's mother-side aunt

Sounds like "ee-moh-boo"

## white (people)

1. 백인 (baekin)

Sounds like "bae-gheen"

## wife

1. 아내 (anae)

Sounds like "ah-nae"

## woman

1. 여자 (yeoja)

Sounds like "yuh-jah"

# Ch. 3 Self Quiz

address

airline

airport

arrival

arrive

bridge

camera

capital city

city

departure

direction

distance

east

East, the

embassy

flight attendant

hotel

ID

immigrant

map

metro

motel

north

passport

pilot

south

tourist

travel

trip

vacation

west

West, the

world

# Ch. 3 Answers

**address**

1. 주소 (juso)

Sounds like "joo-soh"

**airline**

1. 항공 (hanggong)

Sounds like "hahng-gohng"

**airport**

1. 공항 (gonghang)

Sounds like "gohng-hahng"

**arrival**

1. 도착 (dochak)

Sounds like "doh-chahg"

## arrive

1. 도착하다 (dochakhada)

Sounds like "doh-chah-kah-dah"

## bridge

1. 다리 (dari)

Sounds like "dah-ree"

## camera

1. 카메라 (kamera)

Sounds like "kah-meh-rah"

## capital city

1. 수도 (sudo)

Sounds like "soo-doh"

## city

1. 도시 (dosi)

Sounds like "doh-shee"

## departure

1. 출발 (chulbal)

Sounds like "chool-bahl"

## direction

1. 방향 (banghyang)

Sounds like "bahng-hyahng"

## distance

1. 거리 (geori)

Sounds like "guh-ree"

## east

1. 동쪽 (dongjjok)

Sounds like "dohng-jjohng"

## East, the

1. 동양 (dongyang)

Sounds like "dohng-yahng"

## embassy

1. 대사관 (daesagwan)

Sounds like "dae-sah-gwahn"

## flight attendant

1. 승무원 (seungmuwon)

Sounds like "seung-moo-wuhn"

## hotel

1. 호텔 (hotel)

Sounds like "hoh-tehl"

## ID

1. 신분증 (shinbunjeung)

Sounds like "sheen-boon-jjeung"

## immigrant

1. 이주민 (ijumin)

Sounds like "ee-joo-meen"

## map

1. 지도 (jido)

Sounds like "jee-doh"

## metro

1. 지하철 (jihacheol)

Sounds like "jee-hah-chuhl"

## motel

1. 모텔 (motel), general form

Sounds like "moh-tehl"

2. 여관 (yeogwan), alternative form

Sounds like "yuh-gwahn"

## north

1. 북쪽 (bukjjok)

Sounds like "boog-jjohg"

## passport

1. 여권 (yeogwon)

Sounds like "yuh-ggwuhn"

## pilot

1. 조종사 (jojongsa)

Sounds like "joh-johng-sah"

## south

1. 남쪽 (namjjok)

Sounds like "nahm-jjohg"

## tourist

1. 관광객 (gwangwanggaeg), general form

Sounds like "gwahn-gwahng-gaeg"

2. 여행객 (yeohaenggaek), alternative form

Sounds like "yuh-haeng-gaeg"

## travel

1. 여행 (yeohaeng), noun

Sounds like "yuh-haeng"

2. 여행 가다 (yeohaeng gada), verb

Sounds like "yuh-haeng gah-dah"

## trip

1. 여행 (yeohaeng), travel

Sounds like "yuh-haeng"

2. 관광 (gwangwang), sightseeing

Sounds like "gwahn-gwahng"

## vacation

1. 휴가 (hyuga)

Sounds like "hyou-gah"

## west

1. 서쪽 (seojjok)

Sounds like "suh-jjohg"

## West, the

1. 서양 (seoyang)

Sounds like "suh-yahng"


## world

1. 세계 (segye)

Sounds like "seh-gyeah"

# Ch. 4 Self Quiz

adjective

adverb

alphabet

Chinese (language)

definition

dictionary

English (language)

foreign language

French (language)

grammar

greeting

Hindi

Japanese (language)

Korean (language)

language

mean

meaning

native

paragraph

parts of speech

phrase

pronounce

pronunciation

Russian (language)

sentence

sound

Spanish (language)

speak

spell

spelling

translate

translator

vocabulary

**voice**

**word**

# Ch. 4 Answers

## adjective

1. 형용사 (hyeongyongsa)

Sounds like "hyuhng-yohng-sah"

## adverb

1. 부사 (busa)

Sounds like "boo-sah"

## alphabet

1. 문자 (munja)

Sounds like "moon-jjah"

## Chinese (language)

1. 중국어 (junggugeo)

Sounds like "joong-goo-guh"

## definition

1. 정의 (jeongui)

Sounds like "juhng-eui"


## dictionary

1. 사전 (sajeon)

Sounds like "sah-juhn"


## English (language)

1. 영어 (yeongeo)

Sounds like "yuhng-uh"


## foreign language

1. 외국어 (wegugeo)

Sounds like "weh-goo-guh"


## French (language)

1. 프랑스어 (peurangseueo), general form

Sounds like "peu-rahng-sseu-uh"

2. 불어 (buleo), alternative form

Sounds like "boo-ruh"

## grammar

1. 문법 (munbeop)

Sounds like "moon-bbuhb"

## greeting

1. 인사 (insa)

Sounds like "een-sah"

## Hindi

1. 힌디어 (hindieo)

Sounds like "heen-dee-uh"

## Japanese (language)

1. 일본어 (ilboneo)

Sounds like "eel-boh-nuh"

## Korean (language)

1. 한국어 (hangugeo)

Sounds like "hahn-goo-guh"

## language

1. 언어 (eoneo), language in general

Sounds like "uh-nuh"

2. 국어 (gukeo), number of languages/Korean language

Sounds like "goo-guh"

## mean

1. 뜻하다 (tteutada), general form

Sounds like "ddeu-tah-dah"

2. 의미하다 (uimihada), alternative form

Sounds like "eui-mee-hah-dah"

## meaning

1. 뜻 (tteut), general form

Sounds like "ddeut"

2. 의미 (uimi), alternative form

Sounds like "eui-mee"

## native

1. 네이티브 (neitibeu), someone from a specific place

Sounds like "neh-ee-tee-beu"

2. 원어민 (wonamin), someone who is a native speaker

Sounds like "wuh-nuh-meen"

## paragraph

1. 문단 (mundan)

Sounds like "moon-dahn"

## parts of speech

1. 품사 (pumsa)

Sounds like "poom-sah"

## phrase

1. 관용구 (gwanyonggu)

Sounds like "gwah-nyohng-ggoo"

## pronounce

1. 발음하다 (bareumhada)

Sounds like "bah-reum-hah-dah"

## pronunciation

1. 발음 (bareum)

Sounds like "bah-reum"

## Russian (language)

1. 러시아어 (reosiaeo)

Sounds like "ruh-shee-ah-uh"

## sentence

1. 문장 (munjang)

Sounds like "moon-jahng"

## sound

1. 소리 (sori), noun

Sounds like "soh-ree"

2. 소리가 나다 (soriga nada), verb

Sounds like "soh-ree-gah nah-dah"

## Spanish (language)

1. 스페인어 (seupeineo)

Sounds like "seu-peh-ee-nuh"

## speak

1. 말하다 (malhada), say something out loud

Sounds like "mahl-hah-dah"

2. 할 줄 알다 (hal jul alda), speak a language

Sounds like "hahl jjool ahl-dah"

## spell

1. 쓰다 (sseuda)

Sounds like "sseu-dah"

## spelling

1. 스펠링 (seupelling), used for English words

Sounds like "seu-pehl-ling"

2. 맞춤법 (matchumbeop), used for Korean words

Sounds like "maht-choom-bbuhb"

## translate

1. 번역하다 (beonyeokada), translate written words

Sounds like "buh-nyuh-kah-dah"

2. 통역하다 (tongyeokada), interpret languages

Sounds like "tohng-yuh-kah-dah"

## translator

1. 번역가 (beonyeokga), text translator

Sounds like "buh-nyuhg-ggah"

2. 통역사 (tongyeoksa), interpreter

Sounds like "tohng-yuhg-ssah"

## vocabulary

1. 어휘 (eohwi)

Sounds like "uh-hwee"

## voice

1. 목소리 (moksori)

Sounds like "mohg-ssoh-ree"


## word

1. 단어 (daneo)

Sounds like "dah-nuh"

# Ch. 5 Self Quiz

appliance

bag

bicycle

boat

box

comic book

doll

fan

glasses

gun

magazine

motorcycle

newspaper

object

part

radio

scissors

thing

toy

umbrella

watch (thing)

# Ch. 5 Answers

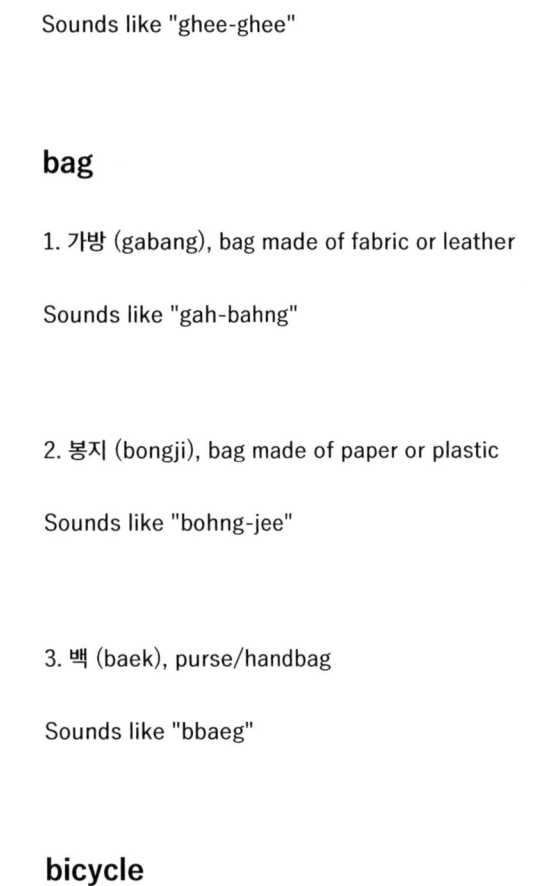

**appliance**

1. 기기 (gigi)

Sounds like "ghee-ghee"

**bag**

1. 가방 (gabang), bag made of fabric or leather

Sounds like "gah-bahng"

2. 봉지 (bongji), bag made of paper or plastic

Sounds like "bohng-jee"

3. 백 (baek), purse/handbag

Sounds like "bbaeg"

**bicycle**

1. 자전거 (jajeongeo)

Sounds like "jah-juhn-guh"

## boat

1. 배 (bae)

Sounds like "bae"

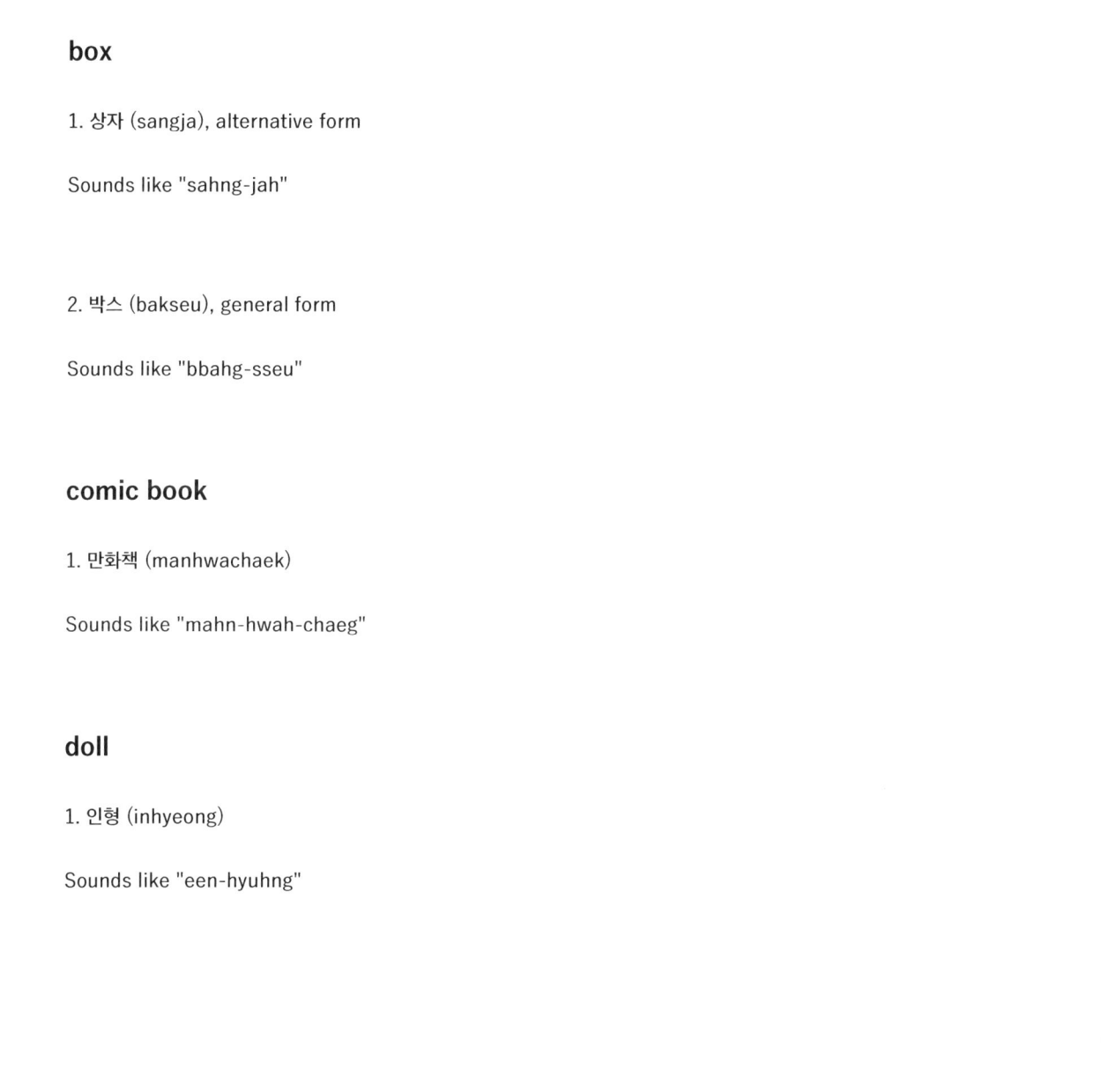

## box

1. 상자 (sangja), alternative form

Sounds like "sahng-jah"

2. 박스 (bakseu), general form

Sounds like "bbahg-sseu"

## comic book

1. 만화책 (manhwachaek)

Sounds like "mahn-hwah-chaeg"

## doll

1. 인형 (inhyeong)

Sounds like "een-hyuhng"

## fan

1. 선풍기 (seonpunggi)

Sounds like "suhn-poong-ghee"

## glasses

1. 안경 (angyeong)

Sounds like "ahn-gyuhng"

## gun

1. 총 (chong)

Sounds like "chong"

## magazine

1. 잡지 (japji)

Sounds like "jahb-jjee"

## motorcycle

1. 오토바이 (otobai)

Sounds like "oh-toh-bah-ee"

## newspaper

1. 신문 (shinmun)

Sounds like "sheen-moon"

## object

1. 물체 (mulche)

Sounds like "mool-cheh"

## part

1. 부분 (bubun)

Sounds like "boo-boon"

## radio

1. 라디오 (radio)

Sounds like "rah-dee-oh"

## scissors

1. 가위 (gawi)

Sounds like "gah-wee"

## thing

1. 물건 (mulgeon)

Sounds like "mool-guhn"


## toy

1. 장난감 (jangnangam), general form

Sounds like "jahng-nahn-ggahm"


2. 토이 (toi), alternative form

Sounds like "toh-ee"


## umbrella

1. 우산 (usan)

Sounds like "woo-sahn"


## watch (thing)

1. 시계 (shigye)

Sounds like "shee-gyeah"

# Ch. 6 Self Quiz

auto

auto insurance

auto mechanic (place)

automobile

car

car accident

crosswalk

diesel

drive

driver

driver's license

gas station

gasoline

GPS system

highway

hood (auto)

insurance

lane (auto)

park (auto)

ride

road

road sign

seat

seatbelt

speed

speed limit

tire

traffic

traffic light

truck

trunk

van

way (auto)

**wheel**

# Ch. 6 Answers

### auto

1. 차 (cha)

Sounds like "chah"

### auto insurance

1. 자동차 보험 (jadongcha boheom)

Sounds like "jah-dohng-chah boh-huhm"

### auto mechanic (place)

1. 자동차 정비소 (jadongcha jeongbiso)

Sounds like "jah-dohng-chah juhng-bee-soh"

### automobile

1. 자동차 (jadongcha)

Sounds like "jah-dohng-chah"

## car

1. 차 (cha), car in general

Sounds like "chah"

2. 승용차 (seungyongcha), sedan

Sounds like "seung-yohng-chah"

## car accident

1. 자동차 사고 (jadongcha sago)

Sounds like "jah-dohng-chah sah-goh"

## crosswalk

1. 횡단보도 (hoengdanbodo), general form

Sounds like "hwehng-dahn-boh-doh"

2. 건널목 (geonneolmok), alternative form

Sounds like "guhn-nuhl-mohg"

## diesel

1. 디젤 (dijel)

Sounds like "dee-jehl"

## drive

1. 운전하다 (unjeonhada)

Sounds like "woon-juhn-hah-dah"

## driver

1. 운전사 (unjeonsa)

Sounds like "woon-juhn-sah"

## driver's license

1. 운전면허증 (unjeonmyeonheojeung)

Sounds like "woon-juhn-myuhn-huh-jjeung"

## gas station

1. 주유소 (juyuso)

Sounds like "joo-you-soh"

## gasoline

1. 휘발유 (hwibalyu), general form

Sounds like "hwee-bahl-lyou"

2. 가솔린 (gasollin), alternative form

Sounds like "gah-sohl-leen"

## GPS system

1. 내비게이션 (naebigeisyeon)

Sounds like "nae-bee-geh-ee-shuhn"

## highway

1. 고속 도로 (gosok doro)

Sounds like "goh-sohg ddoh-roh"

## hood (auto)

1. 본네트 (bonneteu)

Sounds like "bohn-neh-teu"

## insurance

1. 보험 (boheom)

Sounds like "boh-huhm"

## lane (auto)

1. 차선 (chaseon)

Sounds like "chah-suhn"

## park (auto)

1. 주차하다 (juchahada)

Sounds like "joo-chah-hah-dah"

## ride

1. 타다 (tada)

Sounds like "tah-dah"

## road

1. 도로 (doro)

Sounds like "doh-roh"

## road sign

1. 표지판 (pyojipan)

Sounds like "pyoh-jee-pahn"

## seat

1. 좌석 (jwaseok)

Sounds like "jwah-suhg"

## seatbelt

1. 안전벨트 (anjeonbelteu)

Sounds like "ahn-juhn-behl-teu"

## speed

1. 속도 (sokdo)

Sounds like "sohg-ddoh"

## speed limit

1. 제한 속도 (jehan sokdo)

Sounds like "jeh-hahn sohg-ddoh"

## tire

1. 타이어 (taieo)

Sounds like "tah-ee-uh"

## traffic

1. 교통 혼잡 (gyotong honjap)

Sounds like "gyoh-tohng hohn-jahb"

## traffic light

1. 신호등 (shinhodeung)

Sounds like "sheen-hoh-deung"

## truck

1. 트럭 (teureok)

Sounds like "teu-ruhg"

## trunk

1. 트렁크 (teureongkeu)

Sounds like "teu-ruhng-keu"

## van

1. 밴 (baen)

Sounds like "baen"

## way (auto)

1. 길 (gil)

Sounds like "gheel"


## wheel

1. 운전대 (unjeondae), general form of steering wheel

Sounds like "woon-juhn-ddae"


2. 핸들 (haendeul), alternative form of steering wheel

Sounds like "haen-deul"


3. 바퀴 (bakwi), as in "wagon wheel"

Sounds like "bah-kwee"

# Ch. 7 Self Quiz

ambulance

dentist

doctor

drug

emergency

hospital

medical condition

medicine

nurse

pharmacist

pharmacy

pill

prescription

# Ch. 7 Answers

## ambulance

1. 구급차 (gugeupcha), general form

Sounds like "goo-geub-chah"

2. 앰뷸런스 (aembyulleonseu), alternative form

Sounds like "aem-byoul-luhn-seu"

## dentist

1. 치과 (chigwa), dental hospital

Sounds like "chee-ggwah"

2. 치과 의사 (chigwa uisa), doctor of dentistry

Sounds like "chee-ggwah eui-sah"

## doctor

1. 의사 (uisa)

Sounds like "eui-sah"

## drug

1. 약 (yak), pill/medicine

Sounds like "yahg"

2. 마약 (mayak), narcotics

Sounds like "mah-yahg"

## emergency

1. 응급 상황 (eunggeup sanghwang)

Sounds like "eung-geub sahng-hwahng"

## hospital

1. 병원 (byeongwon)

Sounds like "byuhng-wuhn"

## medical condition

1. 질환 (jilhwan)

Sounds like "jeel-hwahn"

## medicine

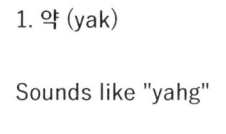

1. 약 (yak)

Sounds like "yahg"

## nurse

1. 간호사 (ganhosa)

Sounds like "gahn-hoh-sah"

## pharmacist

1. 약사 (yaksa)

Sounds like "yahg-ssah"

## pharmacy

1. 약국 (yakguk)

Sounds like "yahg-ggoog"

## pill

1. 알약 (alyak)

Sounds like "ahl-lyahg"

## prescription

1. 처방전 (cheobangjeon)

Sounds like "chuh-bahng-juhn"

# Hangul Pronunciations

## Hangul Consonants

ㄱ = g/k  ㄴ = n  ㄷ = d  ㄹ = l/r  ㅁ = m

ㅂ = b  ㅅ = s/sh  ㅇ = o  ㅈ = j  ㅊ = ch

ㅋ = k  ㅌ = t  ㅍ = p  ㅎ = h  ㄲ = gg/kk

ㄸ = dd/tt  ㅃ = bb  ㅆ = ss  ㅉ = jj


## Hangul Vowels

ㅏ = ah  ㅑ = yah  ㅓ = uh  ㅕ = yuh

ㅗ = oh  ㅛ = yoh  ㅜ = woo  ㅠ = you

ㅐ = ae  ㅒ = yaeh  ㅔ = eh  ㅖ = yeah

ㅘ = wah  ㅙ = wae  ㅚ = weh

ㅝ = wuh  ㅞ = weah  ㅟ = wee

ㅡ = eu  ㅣ = yee  ㅢ = eui

# Word Categories

## Korean Words with Cat Memes 1/5

Basic Pronouns

People

Travel

Languages

Things

Auto

Hospitals & Pharmacies

## Korean Words with Cat Memes 2/5

Basic Verbs

Food & Drinks

Numbers

Places

Time

Colors

Public Transportation

## Korean Words with Cat Memes 3/5

Prepositions & Conjunctions

Houses & Furniture

Arts & Entertainment

Animals & Plants

Days & Dates

Religions

Health

## Korean Words with Cat Memes 4/5

Basic Adjectives

Clothes & Shopping

Weather & Seasons

Money

Phones & Technology

Restaurants

Work

# Korean Words with Cat Memes 5/5

Basic Adverbs

Countries & Nationalities

Education

Body Parts

Nature & Materials

Sports

Miscellaneous

# More Information

## EASY KOREAN

Visit www.easy-korean.com free Korean lessons, dictionary, and more.

## EASY KOREAN on YouTube

Access grammar, listening, vocabulary, and hangul videos for beginners.

## EASY KOREAN on Twitter (@EASY_KOREAN)

Follow EASY KOREAN on Twitter and get the latest updates.

## 9KOREA - Get Korea in English

Visit www.9korea.com for articles and more on living in Korea.

## About the Author

Min Kim is the creator of EASY KOREAN among other projects. He was born in South Korea but spent his teenage years in the United States. He currently lives in Seoul with his two cats, Soomba and Zorro.

If you found this book helpful, please leave a review on the place of purchase. Thank you.

*M.K.*

Made in the USA
San Bernardino, CA
01 December 2018